THE UNNAMED

A WORKBOOK FOR INDIVIDUALS AND SMALL GROUPS

CONTENTS

INTRODUCTION

Noah, The Woman at the Well, Thomas, Hagar; these men and women are more than just names in Bible stories. They were flesh and blood people. And in seeing how God moved in their lives, we can see him moving in ours. We can hear him call us by name.

Named is a 6-week small group resource that tells the story of people from Scripture through a new lens—exploring the mystery of faith with a literary touch. Each series introduces 6 different people from the Bible, unpacking one person's story every week.

This workbook has original stories that are accompanied by historical context for the characters and the times they lived in, insight into how they fit into God's story, and discussion questions to help participants see how God's story works in them. This is a unique opportunity for your group to engage the Scriptures both personally, and as a community. Through the power of history-based stories, you'll see the truth of how God works. Not just in ancient times and in other people, but how he works today and in us all. Become acquainted with the people identified by God in a story as particular as yours.

In this workbook you will find 6 narrative stories about some of those in the Bible who go unnamed. The Unnamed are the unclean, the disabled, the marginalized ones we only know because of Jesus' connection to them. Their names are not known to us, but we know the stories of these outcasts and how Jesus gave them identity.

The narratives are written to help you to begin to think about how these individuals might have been feeling or what they might have been thinking during their story.

Each week before you get together with your group, you might want to read the scriptures that the narrative is based on so that you have a full picture of the story. As you work through the reading and journaling in this book, continue to think about the pieces of the stories that find themselves in your life. What can you learn from these stories and apply in your own life?

CONTEXT

This section will give readers an understanding of what was going on around the person at the time of the story. Historical, societal, and religious background are given to help readers put themselves in the shoes of those whose stories they are about to read.

STORY

The narratives told in this study attempt to get inside the heads of those whose stories we may have heard hundreds of times before. The writers of these pieces have attempted, through research and reflection, to give us a brief glimpse into what these people might have been thinking and how they might have felt. As you read or listen to the story each week look for places where you can relate to the story—God's story.

PLACE IN GOD'S STORY

This section will give you a short description of how God's story found its place in this individual.

THE STORY FINDS ITS PLACE IN ME

These questions are designed to help you reflect on what you've read in order to find yourself in God's narrative. There is plenty of space available for journaling.

Julie Joiner has invested more than eight years writing and editing Sunday School curriculum for Nazarene Publishing House. She earned her BA in writing and literature from Burlington College and MA in counseling from MidAmerica Nazarene University. The roles in which she ministers are intern counselor for New Vision Counseling Center; writer; mom of two grown daughters; and wife of Jim, a man of ministry.

Erina Ludwig is the author of *Unnoticed Neighbors: A Pilgrimage into the Social Justice Story* and writes for the *Indy Star, Indy Spectator,* and *Pattern Magazine.* She holds a history degree from King's College London and was chosen to be one of six European journalists to tour and discuss youth political apathy across the States in 2004 by the U.S. Foreign Press Center. Currently, she is working on her own work of young adult fiction. A Londoner at heart, she now lives in Indianapolis with her husband and their excitable puppy, Lucy.

Annie Carter grew up in Oklahoma with her parents and two older sisters. She holds a BS in Communications and Creative Writing from Olivet Nazarene University in Kankakee, Illinois. Annie has been a student at The Writers Studio in New York since April of 2012. She currently lives in New York City with her cat, Olive.

Joseph Bentz's books span a variety of genres, including a fantasy novel, three contemporary novels, and four nonfiction books on Christian living. His most recent release is *Pieces of Heaven: Recognizing the Presence of God.* Bentz is a professor of English at Azusa Pacific University in Southern California. He lives with his wife and two children in Southern California. His blog, Life of the Mind and Soul, appears at his website, www.josephbentz.com.

THE BENT-OVER WOMAN

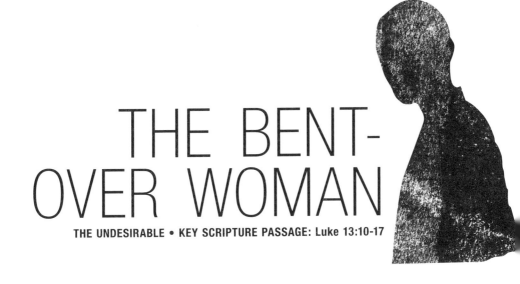

THE UNDESIRABLE • KEY SCRIPTURE PASSAGE: Luke 13:10-17

HER CONTEXT

Ancient Israel was a male-dominated society. A woman's worth was determined by the work she did in the home and the significance of her dowry when given over to a man in marriage. In the days Jesus walked this earth, women had no rights publicly and very few in the privacy of the home. Rabbis of the day determined women were not to be taught, nor were they to be greeted or acknowledged in public. A woman with her hair uncovered in public was likened to a prostitute. To be a woman was such a negative thing that a common proclamation men made in the morning prayers at the synagogue was, "Thank God I am not a woman."

Not only was the culture of this time dominated by men, but it was driven by superstition. People with diseases and deformities were looked upon in judgment, and it was often believed their physical suffering was a result of sin in their lives. The doctors of the times often suggested people bathe in a churning river or practiced bloodletting for healing. Magicians were sought out by pagans in hopes of finding deliverance from physical sufferings.

We do not know the story behind this woman's deformity; all we are given is this: her body had been bent over eighteen years prior by a spirit and she could not stand up straight. This woman, who spent eighteen years of her life bent over and in pain, had little value in a society that considered women possessions to be ruled by men and those with physical handicaps as outcasts.

The Sabbath had long been considered in the Jewish culture more sacred than the needs of human beings. Jesus not only violated the rules of the Sabbath in regard to no work, but He violated the rules of His culture concerning women. He spoke to her and He touched her. Jesus' actions brought attention to this woman as if she were of equal value as a man and of greater value than the traditions of the Sabbath.

HER STORY

It seemed like any other Sabbath as the door latch dropped into place behind her. Though she could not look up into the morning sky, her eyes squinted in adjustment to the bright light. The day was hot. Everything within her wanted to go back inside and curl up on the cool earthen floor and forget about the day. But she moved away from the door. Her contorted body, bent in half, necessitated a slow, cautious pace lest she hazard into something unseen a few feet ahead. Dust clung to her sandals and feet as she shuffled across the street toward the synagogue.

She heard that the Rabbi, Jesus of Nazareth, would be at the synagogue this morning. It seemed everywhere He went people were stirred up like a churning river she once visited in hopes of healing. From what she heard, not one community was left unchanged by Him passing through.

As she shuffled along, she mulled over the conflicting views handed out freely in the marketplace regarding this Rabbi, who claimed to be the Son of God. Some suspected Jesus of leading a rebellion. She recalled voices directed over her—not to her—speaking of broken bodies healed by just a word or touch and captives of darkness untied from bondage.

"I heard my husband talking with some men the other night," one said; "they called Jesus an imposter and all agreed something needed to be done to stop Him."

"It is curious, though," replied another, "how so many of the sick have been made well and demon-possessed set free. Not one of the local healers or magicians helped so many. I have friends who have chosen to follow Him."

The bent woman roamed her imagination, considering the possibilities of Jesus' visit here. "Can any man be so good and powerful?" she thought. "Surely these people exaggerate. I want to see with my own eyes if Jesus is who He claims."

Too late she realized her mistake in getting lost in thought as she walked. She hadn't stopped to rest and was now worried about falling and in need of a rest. Within a hand's reach stood a cart, she grabbed hold of it. Looking from side to side, she gathered images of obstacles standing between her and the synagogue. The donkey tied to the cart twitched a tail scattering flies. "There now," she whispered, "you've been a kind beast to let me take a break here alongside your cart."

Just as she let go of the cart, a gruff voice behind her shouted, "Get away from that animal. Get away, you filthy woman!"

"Her need for hope in something beyond this existence drove her out the door and to the synagogue."

Ashamed and frightened by the cart owner's loud rebuke, she struggled to move away from him as quickly as possible, teetering on the tips of her toes while attempting not to topple over. For eighteen years she had suffered this disdain; it was difficult enough being a woman, but being a disfigured woman was painfully lonely. There had never been a husband; no man would desire her twisted body or be satisfied knowing she was unable to bear children. Every minute the pain in her bulging, knotted back and her crushed ribs pinched her lungs, leaving her short of breath; her other organs groaning to function under the weight of her bent body.

It was all of this, and the emotional pain of rejection, that pulled at her to stay home, but her need for hope in something beyond this existence drove her out the door and to the synagogue. She could barely remember life before a dark spirit bent her body in half. But the memories of those agonizing days as a child, pressing in on her and twisting her out of shape, were ripe for tasting at will.

She was not yet six years old when the gall of death wrenched the joy from her girlish heart. Her mother, from her sickbed, had warned of such and tried to prepare her. She could still hear her father's words spoken minutes after her mother left this world with a last painful gasp.

"Girl, you are in charge of the household chores and your brother now. See to it that your work is done by the end of day."

Day after day she worked from sunup to sundown, and the only words her father spoke to her lashed out at her in anger, driving her like a whip and bleeding her heart of all hope. Her child's body bearing the heavy load of household duties and child care was slowly broken and bent as anger replaced the sad ache. Over time a spirit of darkness bowed her body until she was no longer upright. When her father looked upon her deformed body, his face twisted in disgust. His harshness thickened.

Remembering sent a quiver of shame through her body, and she quickly realized how desperately she needed to find a place to sit down. People brushed past her and loudly emitted their disgust at her presence. She figured she must be just outside the synagogue. Several minutes later she found her way into a corner, left to stand. Not one seat could be found, nor was one willingly given to ease her burden.

Jesus, the one people were murmuring about, stood outside her downcast view, and the crowd of people limited her from turning to take a sideways glance. But an authoritative voice read the Scriptures and drew her attention to this man calling himself the Son of God. Unaware His eyes rested on her distorted body, she heard a gentle, commanding voice say, "Come to Me."

There was a long pause in which thoughts fluttered in her mind, "Is He talking to me? How will I get up there through this crowd without falling over? I can't go in there. Women are forbidden to join the men. Oh, but I must go!"

He did call her to come forward. She picked at thoughts scattered about in her mind as she slowly moved through the crowd. "I can feel eyes looking at me. Are they confused, disgusted, or surprised in anticipation as am I?"

And suddenly she was standing in front of Him. She knew it was so because His sandaled feet came into view. Jesus said to her, "Woman, you are freed from your sickness." Instantly her view changed. Her broken back straightened and she was no longer looking at His sandals but straight into the face of this rabbi from Nazareth. She began praising God for untying and releasing her deformed body. Liberated, she spoke words of praise.

But the now unbent woman's surprises were not over yet. Bound by tradition and laws, the ruler of the synagogue voiced indignation. Directing his comments to the congregants, he spoke out against Jesus taking liberties to heal on the Sabbath.

"There are six days in which work should be done," he argued, "so come during them and get healed, and not on the Sabbath."

The woman would never forget her new view as Jesus replied. "You hypocrites, does not each of you on the Sabbath untie his ox or his donkey from the stall and lead him away to water him? And this woman, a daughter of Abraham as she is, whom Satan has bound for eighteen long years, should she not have been released from this bond on the Sabbath day?"

A collision of views charged the air surrounding the miracle of deliverance from the evil spirit that pressed her down for so many years. But the woman knew how she believed. For too long she was bent toward the ground, unable to see more than snapshots of the space around her. Standing straight before the Son of God, her eyes beheld a panoramic view of her world and a glimpse of eternity.   —JJ

HER PLACE IN GOD'S STORY

In this story we encounter an anonymous woman in a synagogue. All we really know about her is that she was a daughter of Abraham, meaning an Israelite, and she suffered for eighteen years with her body bent over by a spirit. The spirit oppressing her is considered to be an evil spirit. Paul was also tormented by a messenger from Satan for which he had prayed against three times. God allowed this spirit in Paul's life to keep him humble and as a reminder of his dependence on God (2 Corinthians 12:7). The woman of our story today seems to have suffered for another reason.

//She could barely remember life before a dark spirit bent her body in half. But the memories of those agonizing days as a child, pressing in on her and twisting her out of shape, were ripe for tasting at will.**//**

Jesus noticed the woman with the distorted body and called her forward; she did not elicit this attention nor seek His healing touch. The bent woman was merely doing what any Orthodox Jew would do on the Sabbath—attend synagogue. There is no indication she went to synagogue that day in expectation of healing (Luke 13:10-11). Jesus' calling her to Him and touching her was an expression of value of her as a woman, not to mention a handicapped woman. She was not a possession or an outcast to Him, but a person made in the image of God in need of compassion and mercy.

Jesus laid His hands on her and she stood straight. Immediately after her body was made whole, she began glorifying God. Her first response to was to give praise; no longer self-conscious before her community, she glorified God out loud. It was one of many miracles Jesus performed that brought glory to God and revealed Jesus as the Son of God.

A miracle of healing was performed on the bent-over woman on the Sabbath in the synagogue. First, Jesus esteemed this woman by calling her out of the crowd, touching her, and healing her. His actions toward this woman went against the cultural norms. Jesus' actions challenge the inequitable treatment of women, as well as the handicapped of this time.

Jesus exposed the heart of the ruler of the synagogue. In Mark 2:27-28 Jesus responded to the Pharisees' accusation of the disciples' unlawful behavior on the Sabbath with these words, "The Sabbath was made for man, and not man for the Sabbath. So the Son of Man is Lord even of the Sabbath." Jesus exposed the sin of valuing the law at the expense of the woman created in the image of God, the Lawmaker.

THE STORY FINDS ITS PLACE IN ME

1. What parts of The Bent-Over Woman's story find their place in you?

The spirit of anger
Being told how worthless she was
+ Choosing to forgives +
Healing of the heart

2. The bent woman had been unable to straighten herself. For eighteen years she suffered in bondage by a spirit until the words of Jesus spoke deliverance over her. Have you ever been in bondage as a result of something so hurtful that only a word from the Spirit of God could or did set you free?

3. This woman had suffered greatly for eighteen years; she had reason to be bitter and angry. When Jesus told her she was free, she immediately began praising God. How much time do you give to praising and thanking God for His work in your life? Do you make time to be present daily and take notice of all He is doing for you and in you?

4. Right before his eyes a woman was set free from a tortured existence, but the ruler of the synagogue reacted in anger to Jesus' "abuse" of the Sabbath. Jesus' act of mercy exposed the sin in the heart of the official. Is there any viewpoint in your life to which you have become so attached that Jesus cannot do a new thing in you?

5. Has your own suffering or bondage kept you from rejoicing in someone else's deliverance?

NOTES

THE WOMAN
AT THE WELL

THE THIRSTY • KEY SCRIPTURE PASSAGE: John 4:1-26

HER CONTEXT

Although little is known of the exact details of the Samaritan woman's life and history, the long traditions of both Judah and Samaria and their mutual animosity have given us a glimpse into the culture and ways of her world at the time.

From the time Joshua conquered Canaan and divided the land for the tribes of Israel, there had been the northern and southern kingdoms. Around the eighth century BC, Assyria invaded Samaria and over time and generations, the two groups integrated and intermarried turning Sychar into a cosmopolitan, almost pantheistic hub where Jehovah could be found in a temple just streets away from pagan gods.

Thus grew the deep schism between Judah and Samaria and all their generations to come. The rabbis in Jerusalem maintained it was in their temple, where the ark was, that God's holiness abided. Yet, Samaria never relinquished its claim to an ancient spiritual lineage either.

It would have been within that climate that our Samaritan woman would have grown up. We can know of her life as a woman from the Bible—codes that carefully detail a woman's life and what should be done to protect that. It was a patriarchal period, but the rights of widows was one topic that was almost feverishly written about. Whether it was to allow her to collect fallen fruit and grain or for men to fulfill their part of a Levirate marriage, where upon her husband's death his brother was to marry her and bear his deceased brother's children.

This was a time when a woman joined her husband's family, took his name, and merged her identity with his. It was a time when interactions were chaperoned and inspected for any sign of scandal. It would have been a time when few women were known in their own right and/or very rarely remembered for it.

HER STORY

Autumn in Samaria is like no other. The air is finally cooler after the searing burn of summer and the trees bend and sway full of fruit ready to be picked. Baskets brim with lemons, oranges, olives, and pears. They leave their fragrance all over the large open sky. I've seen the seasons change thirty-eight times, and I'm still not tired of the rhythm.

The early morning is the best time. The bustle hasn't begun yet and the moon and the sun are still vying over who should give the light. I take my shawl from the back of the front door and look at the hinges that are about to come loose. I won't grumble, not today, not this morning.

I walk the uneven path I have walked a hundred—a thousand—times before. I could do this with my eyes closed. I start to climb and my breath becomes shorter, but I won't stop, I won't be late. When I arrive, no one is there and yet as I look at the brilliant white limestone rocks, I sense the presence of so many others. I nearly miss the new small grave for the Haddassi girl. She lived only a week before she returned to dust.

It has been twenty years, but every image is still as clear as cut glass. My heart whispers, "Jacob," but I won't speak, because if I do, I know I'll cry and once I do, I won't stop.

We were young when we married. I was fifteen and he was eighteen. We barely knew each other. We were both our parents' choices. When he carried me home, I cried for my mother and my own bed and he held me and let me weep.

We shared good first years and when I turned eighteen, I found out we were expecting our first child. I can still see the light in his face when I told him. The sun had given him creases, but they only made his dimples deeper. He had plans for us, and he boasted about them to everyone, especially his brothers.

I kneel now, in front of his stone and I take out the small box I have brought along and lift the lid. The myrrh is strong and thick and heavily fragrant. I bow and say my prayers. I pray to remember him, I pray to remember us, and I pray to remember joy.

* * *

I'm back before he awakes, which is good, because last night he drank too much and laughed too much and today he'll be bitter and full of regret.

I make tea and stand aside and wait.

Even after all that wine, he still rises like clockwork. He slumps onto the low stool and tears at the bread. He slurps his tea and smacks his lips together and apart.

"So, you went to talk with the dead, I see." But he doesn't see. He doesn't even look at me. He just chews noisily.

I say nothing and keep my eyes trained on a line of grain along the wall that means we have mice again.

"Ah, so you will not speak to me. Must I die first?" He looks up this time and his eyes are large and bloodshot.

"It is the anniversary of his death," I whisper. I can't talk any louder. Even if I wanted to, my mouth is parched.

"Jacob," he spits. "Must I always hear his name?"

"I didn't say his name."

He looks up amused and surprised, "We *are* bold now." He stands up and lets his full height fill the room. He glares down at me and for a moment; I think his words will turn into fists.

"The jars are empty, I need to wash." He starts back to bed. I have my orders.

* * *

I walk until the town becomes small yellow bricks behind me. There is a closer well, but the water here is sweeter. No wonder my forefathers drank from it. And today it brings me closer to my Jacob.

When I arrive it is burning hot. Even in autumn, the noonday sun is sharp and unforgiving. I'm always alone at this time; no one with the slightest bit of sense would do such heavy manual labor at this hour. But it feels safe. Every now and again I try to join the other women when the sun isn't so high. It's nice to hear their stories, the news and see the children play, but the deathly silence as I lower my pail makes me grieve for weeks afterward.

It wasn't always like this. I wasn't always this.

"Will you give me a drink?" He sits on the other side of the well's wall and He's a Jew. His clothes, His accent, His mannerisms; everything about Him says, "Judah."

It's hard not to be surprised; this never happens.

"Why are you, a Jewish man, asking me, a Samaritan woman, for a drink?" I chuckle now, amused. Perhaps the heat has gotten to Him. His feet are incredibly dusty and His robes are tinted reddish brown. His brown hair is thick and curly, but it's damp in places and stuck to His face.

"If only you knew what gift God has for you and you knew who was talking to you, you'd be asking me for a drink and you would get living water." He says this calmly and His steady eyes never leave my face, but it still irks me. I nearly drop my bucket down the well.

"And how do you suppose to get that water? With your hands?" I laugh again. "You're a stranger in these parts. Living water . . ." I shake my head. "Do you think you can do better than our father, Jacob?" And there it is, I've said his name, and though it is not *my* Jacob, my mouth dries. The name sticks in my throat and starts to choke me.

"This water will leave you thirsty," the man says, looking down the well. "If you drink the water I give, you'll never be thirsty again. The water I give will be like a spring of water welling up to eternal life."

I focus on Him again and He's looking intently at me, but patiently. He shields His eyes from the sun so He can see me.

"I would like that water. I would like never to be thirsty again," I say quietly.

He drops His hand. "Go and get your husband and come back."

I flush and I know my face is burning red. News travels fast, it seems. I think of the sleeping man back at home and the lot I've been given.

"I don't have a husband."

"You are honest," He says softly. "You've had five husbands and this last one isn't yours."

All is still for a moment. Not many people know, but sometimes there is the coolest of breezes that blows over this well at this burning hour. It's as if it is a balm to our sores and it soothes any fever.

"But it's not as they think," He says, and I know He means the community that has shunned me.

"What is a woman, without a man to guard her?" I ask, thinking of Aaron, the man in my home.

The man stands up off the wall and lays His hands on my shoulders. "You were not to blame."

I know He's talking about Jacob, the day he went to work when I was carrying his child and never came home. He's talking about how he fell, because he was so tired from working so many hours for more money for us. He's talking about how I came and held his head in my lap and begun to mourn a death I could never recover from. Not after losing our child, nor marrying his brother, nor after marrying his other brothers who soon discarded me.

The man by the well doesn't say any of these things, but I can see He understands more than any other, that when Jacob died, I did too.

"So you're a prophet," I say, and we talk about the great divide between our people. There is a Messiah, and when He comes, He'll make everything clear," I say, thinking of childhood prayers.

A small bird shoots by, very close to His face, but He doesn't flinch.

"The one talking to you is He." He doesn't crow these words proudly, nor is He loud, He merely makes a statement.

My pail has slipped out of my hands and I hear it splash into the water below. I'm looking at Him for a slight crack, for any falsehood, but all I see is a depth and generosity that makes Him true. And inside, my heart swells with fear and gladness.

—EL

HER PLACE IN GOD'S STORY

Most people immediately praise the Samaritan woman's evangelical zeal after speaking to Jesus, but when she first hears His offer of "living water," she is fast to quip about the logistical difficulty of His words without a bucket. It illustrates not only her childlike understanding but also a frankness and human honesty in the face of Jesus' mysterious wording (John 4:10-12).

It becomes apparent in their conversation, that despite or maybe because of her history, she still has plenty of faith. Within a few minutes, this woman fully embraces His disclosure of being the Messiah she has been waiting for. (John 4:28-29, NIV).

During this brief meeting, Jesus faces and undoes two huge issues: gender and race. It is Jesus who initiates the conversation challenging most of the day's protocol. She is at the well around nooon, which highlights her pariah existence in the community, and she is carrying the water herself, perhaps indicating she is without the assistance most women would have had in their homes. Also, she is a

Samaritan, and Samaritans were at historical odds with the Jews. He talks to her with such directness and yet, without condemning. Even His disciples are surprised to find them alone (John 4:17-27).

The Orthodox Church calls the Samaritan woman Photina, which means "light." In some Christian traditions she has become a saint for her ready faith in Jesus and her eagerness to tell her community that she had met the man who knows everything about her (John 4:29-30).

When Jesus declared, "I who speak to you am he" (John 4:26, NIV), her passionate response is remembered, but little has been said of her courage. She returned to her town to face and tell the neighbors who had most likely left her on the fringes of their lives, that the Christ was here (John 4:28-30, 39). It was because of her willingness to be brave that many were saved (John 4:41).

THE STORY FINDS ITS PLACE IN ME

1. What parts of The Woman at the Well's story find their place in you?

2. The Samaritan woman speaks her mind in all simplicity and honesty when talking with Jesus. Have you spoken without clichés and been frank about your doubts and confusion?

3. During the conversation, the Samaritan woman becomes fixed on her ethnic and religious background to validate herself. How often do you use culture, history, and experiences in your life as a divide against God?

4. The woman declares her belief in a Messiah and waits for Him to come. Do you think we still crave a superhero to be amongst us? For demigods with blazing power to protect, speak up for, love, notice, and choose us?

5. The story ends with 'Photina' heading back into her community and facing those who may have made her life difficult to share a message of hope with them. Would you be prepared to head into the fray, be it your workplace, family or elsewhere, to see their burdens lifted by one who can? What might keep you from doing so?

NOTES

THE GOOD SAMARITAN

THE UNLIKELY • KEY SCRIPTURE PASSAGE: Luke 10:25-37

HIS CONTEXT

At this point in history, Jews and Samaritans notoriously hated one another. It was a dispute rooted in their ancestry. The implication at the time was that Samaritans were transplants from Kuthah (Kuthim) and therefore had no claim to their Jewish heritage. This matter of origin became grounds for a long and violent history of hate and segregation between the two groups. So much so that, after the death of King Solomon, the entire nation of Israel split in two with Jerusalem as one capital and Samaria as the other. Historically, this split was a kind of catalyst for an endless political and religious tug of war that we still see today.

This divisiveness was so extreme that, by the time Jesus arrives, you would be hard-pressed to find a group more rejected by the Jews than Samaritans or perhaps lepers. This backdrop, along with a pervasive allegiance to the religious laws of the day, sets the stage for one of the most widely known parables taught by Jesus in the Bible.

HIS STORY

He thought of his mother. It was a strange last thought. The man hadn't seen his mother for the better part of ten years. From where he lay on the ground, he could see the sun was setting. If he were still a boy, his mother would have wondered where he was and she would have taken a switch to him for being late to supper. He started to weep. He wished he could see his mother. The man wondered now if his reasons for leaving Jerusalem were really so important that he should have left at all.

Belly up in the gravel, the man could feel his blood pooling all around him. Cold was coming up from the canyons. The ground sloped away from him into a gully to his right, and he expected that was where he'd end up. He shuddered at the humiliation of dying without a burial. His head tilted over and the sculptural ridges of the rising rock wall beside him swirled and swayed. Everything seemed to expand. His sense of time diluted like pigment dropped into water. He had only seen two figures pass since the thieves left him to die where he was, and that could have been hours ago. The way they looked at him when they passed, like when women cover their children's eyes in the presence of a drunk. The passersby treated him like a person to be ignored for fear of what might happen to you if you encounter them. And yet in this last moment he felt something like being fully sane in a way he had not known existed.

He tried to focus his eyes, but everything swam around him in milky blue. The thieves had not even left him his tallit, and he knew he would not be touched once it was night. Cool air blew over him, and his naked body throbbed with a kind of numbness. Would the sense of pain be keener if there were someone beside him to bear witness? He took in breath once or twice and willed his right arm to move. His fingers rose and his arm slowly glided out from his body; he felt dust and stones move under his palm. The effort was exhausting, and he was still a moment.

As it turned out, there was weightlessness to dying. The ground under him seemed to be trying to rise up to meet him from where he hovered just above earth. A shiver went from his shoulders to his wrists. Such was death. An unraveling at his fingertips and that was all. He felt an almost sense of relief. All this living must have been preparation to die, and now he was through with the terrible waiting. He took in a slow breath through his nose to smell what grew around him and then let his eyes close. From somewhere in the canyon a crane let out a call, and the sounds of night birds and the hum of locusts ebbed him into eternity.

"Kuthim, he pushed out between broken teeth. The man immediately regretted this slander and raised his hand feebly to the rider's face but could only manage to take hold of the thick, drooping beard. The rider watched him struggle and then took the man firmly by the wrist and held him that way staring quietly into the man's face.*"*

In the stillness he thought he heard a voice—his little brother calling his name. The man opened his eyes and saw an animal stopped on the far side of the road. The rider came off of the donkey and looked left and right and then crossed the road to where the man lay. The rider knelt by the man, laid his satchel to his side, and pushed the white linen back from his forehead to see the man better. The retreating light shaded the rider's already dark eyes until they nearly disappeared into shadow. The man did not recognize this rider, but something in his waning mind reacted to the face. He could not find the word for it.

The rider took up his outer garment and rent it into a long panel at the hem. He bent over the man and tucked the bandage behind his rib cage and wound it around his chest once and then tied it off tightly. He took flat bread from his satchel and broke it apart and held it out to the man. It came to the man now. He knew what this rider was.

Kuthim, he pushed out between broken teeth. The man immediately regretted this slander and raised his hand feebly to the rider's face but could only manage to take hold of the thick, drooping beard. The rider watched him struggle and then took the man firmly by the wrist and held him that way staring quietly into the man's face.

The rider set the man's arm to his side and, as if nothing had been said at all, went back to his task. He took a wineskin from the satchel, uncorked it, and poured the contents out over the man's body. There was a sting as it washed across his belly and thighs, and the man's eyes welled. All around him the air saturated with the sweet scent of wine and from somewhere in his cognitive mind he started to salivate. The man closed his eyes and the hot tears burned when they ran in a deep gash under his left cheek.

A shiver ran through the man, and he opened his eyes to see that the rider had stood and returned to his donkey. Panic took him. He clutched dirt in his hands and tried to lift his knees but his legs fell again. He was so sore he gave out a small cry. He was catching his breath when the rider came quickly back across the road with the donkey beside him led by a length of cord. They stopped directly over the man. The rider took the blanket from the donkey's back and laid it over the man and knelt back down near his face. The man tried to speak again. He opened his mouth and whispered as best he could. *Baruch. Baruch dayan emet.* (Blessed. Blessed is the True Judge.) The funeral prayer hung lifeless in the air. The rider shook his head and looked back over both shoulders and told the man not to be afraid. The man pleaded with him to stay. It was getting dark.

The rider spoke for the first time. "You find it so hard to believe."

"The Samaritan gripped the man in his arms and lifted him from the mire and set him on the donkey. Though they went through the valley to Jericho, the man was no longer afraid in the company of this rider and his foal.**"**

The rider put his right hand behind the man's head and his left arm under the bare legs and steadied himself to rise. The man felt overcome with nausea and tried to lean away. The rider sat back on his knees and tilted the man to one side and the man wretched a few times. The sick was strangely thick and tinny in his mouth. He rolled over into the rider's lap and curled up there like an infant and wept. He considered it grace enough that he would not have to die alone after all, even if it was with this Samaritan. Light paled to a green when the sun dropped past the horizon. In this state of surrender, the Samaritan gripped the man in his arms and lifted him from the mire and set him on the donkey. Though they went through the valley to Jericho, the man was no longer afraid in the company of this rider and his foal.

—AC

HIS PLACE IN GOD'S STORY

This parable could just have easily had the characters swapped. For the Jewish man asking Jesus the question, it may have made more sense for the beaten man on the ground to have been a despised Samaritan and the hero of the story to have been Jewish. But it is no mistake that Jesus chooses his characters so carefully. We are made to identify with the bleeding man on the ground. And though help comes to us from an unlikely place, there is no denying that we have been loved. It is at this point that Jesus tells us, "Go and do the same."

Additionally, it was St. Augustine who likened the parable to the story of Christ himself. There is imagery to the story that parallels Christ's own act of salvation for us broken sinners. We are shown at every turn of the Samaritan's story what love in its truest form really looks like.

It is important to remember that the parable of the Good Samaritan is told by Jesus in a response to the question: What must I do to enter heaven? This is argu- ably the ultimate question of the Bible. It is safe to say, then, that Jesus' answer to this question is a sort of culmination of everything He came to earth to share and every hope of salvation. Therefore, the truths revealed in this parable become essential to our very being as Christ followers.

In essence, the entire Gospel story gets distilled down to this simple element: loving compassion. Such will be the fruit of our faith, and it is this understanding that elevates verses like James 1:27 and 1 John 3:17 to an unmatched importance.

And even more glorious still is the realization in all of this that we have already been subject to this example of compassion. That as sinners saved by grace, we were scooped up off the ground moments before death and carried from harm and made whole once more.

THE STORY FINDS ITS PLACE IN ME

1. What parts of the Good Samaritan's story find their place in you?

2. Consider your routine on any given day. Where are your opportunities to effectively exercise compassion to those around you?

3. Consider if Jesus were using this parable in our modern times. What divisive groups might He have to use to illustrate His point? How might you ensure that the compassion He implores us to make part of our lives does not come with exceptions, in the giving or the receiving?

4. In this narrative of the classic parable, the wounded man could hardly believe that this Samaritan—a people he'd probably always disliked—would be so kind as to help him when others weren't. What ideas do you hold of people in your life that might make it difficult for you to believe good of them?

NOTES

THE MAN
BORN BLIND

THE SEER • KEY SCRIPTURE PASSAGE: John 9:1-12

HIS CONTEXT

One of the objections the Pharisees have to Jesus' healing of the blind man is that it happened on the Sabbath. Specifically, Jesus' making of the mud would have been considered "work" and would have violated Sabbath law. To the legalistic religious leaders, that technical violation of the rules was more important than the miraculous healing of a blind man. Accounts of Jesus healing blindness appear not only in this story, from John 9:1—10:21, but also in the other Gospels (Matthew 9:27-31; Mark 10:46-52; Luke 18:35-43).

The story of the healing of the man born blind takes place only months before Jesus' crucifixion, and the opposition to Him from the Jewish authorities was strong and growing more intense. As Stephen S. Kim explains, "The leaders who vehemently opposed Jesus' healing the paralytic on the Sabbath in John 5 resumed their opposition to Jesus here. In these chapters, however, the opposition to Jesus increased from hostility to hatred, and even intent to murder." Kim points out that in chapters 7 and 8 of John, four mentions are made of Jewish leaders trying to arrest Jesus (7:30, 32, 44; 8:20), and there are three other references to their desire to kill Him (7:1, 19, 25; 8:37). So by the time of the healing in chapter 9, they are looking for any excuse to accuse Jesus of misdeeds.

Like the blind man, Jewish Christians at the time the book of John was written also felt shut out and discriminated against by the Jewish religious leaders. Therefore, the original Christian readers of this story would have easily related to this story of the outcast blind man and his religious oppressors.

HIS STORY

I heard rumors about Jesus, none of them good. He was dangerous. He was espousing all kinds of radical ideas. Some even claimed He was of the devil.

Even before I met Him, I was skeptical of those malicious stories. I was more inclined toward the rumors that people had the courage only to whisper, like maybe He was a prophet, maybe even the Messiah. He did miracles, healing people and freeing people from demons. As a blind man, I was attentive to anything that even hinted at healing. Nothing I had ever tried had worked, but I still fantasized what it must be like to see.

Most of the Pharisees and other Jewish authorities didn't like Jesus, and all but the bravest people were afraid to cross those powerful men and give Jesus a chance. I didn't like the Pharisees, and they certainly had no use for me, a man blind from birth, which to them meant only one thing: I was steeped in sin. So be it. I stayed away from them, and I stayed away from Jesus. If any of them wanted to give me a few coins, I would be grateful. Otherwise, they were not my problem.

Then came the day when I could no longer avoid Jesus *or* the Pharisees. As I sat begging in my usual filthy spot by a wall along a busy road close to the temple, Jesus walked right up to me. I don't know why He stopped and focused on me. Most people ignored me. I heard a big crowd pushing in all around Him. I expected the whole big group to pass me by pretty quickly. I hoped only for a coin or two from some of them.

Instead, Jesus stopped, and so did everybody else. I didn't welcome the attention. When any powerful person paid attention to me, it usually meant trouble. They usually yelled at me to get out of the way or move along to a different spot.

Jesus didn't say anything at first, but then one of His disciples, who was probably also confused about why they had suddenly stopped to stare at a blind man, asked, "Rabbi, who sinned, this man or his parents, that he was born blind?"[1]

That seemed like rather a rude question, considering that I was sitting right there, but it was nothing compared to other things people sometimes said.

I expected Jesus to agree with their idea that sin caused my blindness. I've been hearing that all my life. Instead, He gave an answer that I loved. He said, "Neither this man nor his parents sinned, but this happened so that the work of God might be displayed in his life. As long as it is day, we must do the work of him who sent me. Night is coming, when no one can work. While I am in the world, I am the light of the world."[2]

Ha! I wanted to shout. Finally, somebody not blaming me for being blind. I was ready to stand up and cheer Him right then! Everybody was talking over everybody else in response to what He said, so nobody bothered to ask me what I thought. And honestly, in my own mind I couldn't get past "neither this man nor his parents sinned." I had no idea what He meant by my blindness happening so that the work of God could be displayed or the part about His being the light of the world.

> **"I just looked at their mouths moving as the words formed and thought, so *that's* what faces look like?"**

Before I could think through any of that, He leaned down right in front of me. He spat in the dirt right there by the road and made little globs of mud out of it. Then He reached up and spread it over my eyes. Did He really mean to heal me? Did He have the power?

I hoped that His next words would be, "Now open your eyes and see," but instead He told me to go wash in the pool of Siloam. I had been there before, a number of times over the years, with no results. Still, I hurried over to it, with help from friends who led me. I had quite a following that day because Jesus, whatever else people thought of Him, was famous for His healing.

I will never forget that first moment of sight as the water washed over my face. The dazzling light! It was so different from what I expected. I looked all around me at these patches of light everywhere, the moving greens and blues and reds and yellows. I couldn't believe it. The men kept asking me, "Can you see? Can you see?" But I couldn't answer at first. I just looked at their mouths moving as the words formed and thought, so *that's* what faces look like? So different from how they *feel.* I guess the look on my own face made it clear that I was seeing because one of the men started shouting, "He's healed! He can see!"

My first thought was to go to my parents and neighbors and tell them what happened. My friends had to guide me there because, even though I could see, I didn't know how to get there by *sight,* and all those shapes and colors were so confusing to me for a while that I had to close my eyes sometimes to reorient myself to reality as I understood it.

People at home celebrated with me—at first. Friends and relatives came running to my parents' home when they heard the news. But as word spread about my healing, a more ominous attitude took hold among some of the people in the neighborhood. One of my father's friends told him that some people were spreading rumors that the miracle hadn't really happened. They said I wasn't the same man who had been blind all his life! I was an impostor.

I could hardly keep from laughing at the absurdity of it. Some of these people had known me all my life, and now they weren't sure it was me? Were people really that afraid of the religious authorities?

Finally someone came and told me I would have to go see the Pharisees. So off to the Pharisees I went, hoping to get it over with quickly. But part of me also thought that eventually common sense would prevail, and that even these stern men would say, "Wait, a beautiful thing has happened here!"

In fact, my session with the Pharisees started out bad and only got worse. Even though a couple of them tried to at least acknowledge the possibility that what Jesus did for me was a miracle from God, most of them refused to acknowledge the miracle. As they were questioning me, one of them asked if I thought

Jesus was a sinner. I answered, "Whether he is a sinner or not, I don't know. One thing I do know. I was blind but now I see!"

They all started talking at once, calling me names and threatening me. "We are disciples of Moses," they said. "We don't even know where he comes from."

"You don't know where he comes from, yet he opened my eyes! God doesn't listen to sinners, does he? If Jesus were not from God, he couldn't have done this."

That was more than the bully could take. "You were steeped in sin at birth!" he shouted. "How dare you lecture us!" And he tossed me out.

Getting kicked out at least should have put a stop to all the harassing questions and insults, but on my way home, I had to listen to even more complaints from my family and friends. Why had I offended those men? What would they do to us now? On and on they griped. In the meantime, shimmering daggers of sunlight poked through the leaves of a tree by the side of the road. I was the only one who noticed. All these people supposedly could see, but really they were blind. I didn't want to answer any of their complaints except to say, "Look! That tree is blazing with light!"

Then to the surprise of all of us, we looked up and saw Him standing there in the road. Jesus. Someone had told Him what happened. Since He hadn't come to the pool of Siloam, I still had never seen Him before, but I *knew* it was Him. His disciples trailed behind Him, and some Pharisees and onlookers too. He stared right at me.

"Do you believe in the Son of Man?" He said.

"Who is he, sir?" I asked, feeling suddenly shy. "Tell me so that I may believe in him."

Jesus held out His arms and smiled. "You have now seen him. . . . He is the one speaking with you."

" I will never forget that first moment of sight as the water washed over my face. The dazzling light! It was so different from what I expected. I looked all around me at these patches of light everywhere, the moving greens and blues and reds and yellows. I couldn't believe it. **"**

In that instant, just as the waters of Siloam had washed away my blindness, Jesus' presence washed away my unbelief. I fell at His feet, overcome with joy and gratitude. "Lord," I said, "I believe."

—JB

HIS PLACE IN GOD'S STORY

The healing of the man born blind in John 9 continues two themes that are foreshadowed in the chapters leading up to it: water and light. In chapters 7 and 8, Jesus takes part in the Feast of Tabernacles. John 7:37 says, "On the last and greatest day of the Feast, Jesus stood and said in a loud voice, 'If a man is thirsty, let him come to me and drink. Whoever believes in me, as the Scripture has said, streams of living water will flow from within him'" (NIV). In John 8:12, Jesus says to the people, "I am the light of the world. Whoever follows me will never walk in darkness, but will have the light of life" (NIV).

Just before Jesus makes the mud to spread on the blind man's eyes, He says, "While I am in the world, I am the light of the world" (John 9:5, NIV). Then He sends the man to the pool of Siloam. Jesus is the light to this man, both physically as he washes in the water of Siloam and receives his sight, and also spiritually when he later falls down to worship Jesus and declares his belief in Him.

Many of the people in this story, including the blind man's parents, seem very afraid to offend the Jewish religious leaders by celebrating Jesus' miracle. The healed man becomes increasingly bold as the authorities question him about Jesus, and then they expel him from their presence. The consequences could be dire. As Everett Falconer Harrison explains, "This was only a preliminary expulsion, but there was every prospect that the Sanhédrin itself would confirm the verdict and make it permanent. He was a brave man indeed who would dare for the sake of conviction to face the prospect of being banned from the spiritual privileges and fellowships of his people, and even from the opportunity to make a living, to be treated like a leper the rest of his days." Motivated by gratitude for what Jesus has done for him, the healed man speaks out for his healer in spite of the risks.

THE STORY FINDS ITS PLACE IN ME

1. What parts of The Man Born Blind's story find their place in you?

2. When the disciples first encounter the blind man, they want to ask a theological question about him, but Jesus deflects that and heals him instead. What can we learn from this? Can you think of situations in which it is easy to forget about the human beings involved and focus instead on people only in ideological or theological ways? What can we do to keep the concern for the *person* more central, as Jesus did?

3. As he is being questioned, the man healed from blindness says of Jesus, "Whether he is a sinner or not, I don't know. One thing I do know. I was blind but now I see!" (John 9:25, NIV). This statement becomes true for him not only physically but also spiritually. Does this describe your own spiritual journey? In what ways has Jesus moved you from spiritual blindness to sight?

4. Because of fear, the neighbors and even parents of the formerly blind man seem reluctant to state the obvious. They are afraid to admit the great thing Jesus has done because of the high price they might have to pay for that admission. Is it still hard to take a stand for Jesus? What are some negative repercussions that still can happen? Have you faced this? What gives you the courage to stand up for Jesus even in the face of opposition?

5. "The Man Born Blind" is a story in which people are trying to figure out who Jesus is and what they should do about Him. In your own life, what are the varieties of stances that people you know take toward Jesus? Do you know people who are hostile toward Him? Indifferent? Curious? How can you best lead people toward the truth about Him?

NOTES

THE GADARENE DEMONIAC

THE DELIVERED • KEY SCRIPTURE PASSAGE: Luke 8:26-39

HIS CONTEXT

There is dispute over exactly where the story of the Gadarene demoniac took place. Various biblical accounts locate the story in the country of the Gadarenes or Gerasenes or Gergesenes. Wherever the precise location, it is in Gentile territory.

Some commentators see political satire in the text. The people were living under Roman domination, so perhaps it is significant that the demons have a name associated with the Roman military, "legion." They are also cast into a herd of animals the Jews consider unclean, pigs. "Legion" could simply mean that there are many demons, but as Teresa Calpino points out, "If the author of the story wanted only to express the large number of demons that possess the man . . . why does he use a Latin loanword with such clear connections to the military force of Rome when there are numerous other linguistic choices at his disposal?" Also, like the Romans, the demons don't want to be sent "out of the country." Roman soldiers were also known for eating pork and sacrificing pigs to their gods. Pigs move in an orderly fashion like marching soldiers. It would be easy for a Jewish/Christian audience to enjoy seeing Legion go over the cliff the way the pigs do. It would also be easy for that audience to associate Satan's regime with the Roman one.

Other commentators find an ironic humor in this story. Jesus lets the demons go into the pigs, but then the pigs go over the cliff, so the outcome certainly isn't what the demons desired. The townspeople certainly see nothing funny in these events, nor are they able to see anything positive in it. They ignore the fact that a man has been miraculously restored. Instead of celebrating with him, they react in fear and anger. Although they have the Son of God in their midst, willing to heal and restore and teach them, they only want Him to leave.

People today also respond to Jesus with a similar range of reactions, from gratitude to fear and hostility. He still reaches out in love, but only some are willing to receive.

HIS STORY

My life was torment. My highest aspiration was death. Wild ideas like happiness or wholeness were so beyond the realm of my existence that I never even bothered to hope for them. Demon-possessed, I lived among the tombs, naked and raving.

I once lived in the village like everyone else. I was a beloved son. I worked for my father, tending our animals. I had brothers and sisters and cousins. I had dignity. I lost everything. Now the townspeople only wanted me out of the way. Even my family had given up on me. I was an embarrassment. They couldn't stand to look at me or hear my voice or even to remember that I existed. Instead of clothing, my body was covered only with dirt, scabs, and bruises.

I sensed Jesus coming toward me well before I could see Him. The power in Him, the threat, radiated through the ground like an earthquake. I was alarmed, and the demons inside me were filled with such rage that I flung myself down on the ground immediately and writhed in the dirt and rocks.

Maybe I should say *they* flung me down, but part of my agony was that I no longer knew my own identity. Was I *me,* or was I *them*? It didn't make much difference as I rolled on the ground *hoping* to hurt myself, *desiring* to feel the sharp rocks slice my already seared flesh. Nothing out there ever brought me relief, but sharp physical pain came the closest because it was a temporary distraction from my spiritual torment.

The terror inside me kept building as we felt Jesus approaching, but when I stood up and actually saw Him across the horizon, surrounded by His entourage and a gathering of curious townspeople, I thought my body would rip into shreds with the fury of it. I ran toward Him, not because I wanted to, but because everything inside me propelled me in that direction.

People scattered when I came near. They pulled their loved ones away from the naked, bleeding man. More than any other humiliation I suffered, the *looks* from other people were what I dreaded most and yet I couldn't blame them. To most of them I was a monster, not a human being. They looked at me with disgust. One man threw a rock at me and yelled, "Get away!" as if I were a wild animal.

That's why I no longer minded living among the tombs. It was a relief to be away from all the abuse and stares. For a long time my family tried to keep me in the village. They hid me at home at first, not sure of what was wrong with me, hoping I would recover. Finally I got so violent and they got so scared that they made shackles and bound me with chains. But by then, with what was inside me, I was so strong and so violent that I could break every fetter and every chain they put on me. I would wrench it right off, to their amazement. Then I would fly into rages and smash up tables and chairs and jars and pots, anything I could get my hands on. It was intolerable, not only to my own family but to the whole town, so they banished me to the tombs.

I can't blame them for what they did, but it was still cruel. I wanted them to kill me, but I don't think they wanted to take responsibility for going that far. They hoped I would kill myself, and I would have if what lived inside me had let me do it. The tombs were the right place for me. Everybody wanted me dead, so why not start living among the dead now.

The men around Jesus tried to push me away. They didn't want someone like me touching Him. But Jesus brushed them aside, as if I were exactly the person He had come to see, and He stood inches away from me. My insides burned as if I had swallowed hot coals. I writhed in pain. I fell on my knees, unable to stand. Jesus stood still, calm, focusing His eyes directly on me in a way no one else ever did.

"What do you want with me, Jesus, Son of the Most High God?" I heard myself shout. I knew that's who He was, knew it without being told, knew it before I even saw Him.

"Come out of this man, you evil spirit," Jesus said, and my head spun in dizzying confusion. I grabbed my head to try to keep it from splitting apart. "What is your name?"

"My name is Legion," I heard myself say, "for we are many."

Then, in the midst of my nauseating disorientation that made it hard to know what anyone was doing or saying, I found myself begging Jesus not to send us out of the area, but to send us into the pigs nearby. We were trying to survive. But already I knew, I could *feel,* that *I* wasn't begging for this. *They* were begging. Legion.

Everybody around Jesus stood silent, riveted. They waited for His response.

He spoke a word—I was too overwhelmed to hear it—and they went out of me. I fell to the ground, depleted, incapable of moving.

"I hovered nearby, so grateful and stunned by what had happened to me. I wanted nothing else from Him."

Now everyone's attention turned to the pigs. There must have been hundreds of them, being tended just beyond us. They were clustered near a cliff that dropped down toward the lake. Within seconds of Jesus' speaking, the animals ran about wildly, spinning in every direction, running into one another, biting and jumping on the other pigs. There was nothing for the men tending them to do but get out of the way, because every pig in that herd now was determined to run off that cliff and fall to their deaths below.

The only one who paid them no attention was Jesus. He kept His eyes right on me, and when the worst was over, He smiled at me. I could not even remember the last time I had seen a smile directed my way.

The next few hours were chaos, with everybody yelling about the pigs and running to town to spread the word and trying to figure out what to do. Jesus ignored all the yelling and took care of me, as if I were His sole reason for coming to this village. With each act of kindness from Jesus and His followers, I felt the humanity seep back into me.

In spite of what happened with the pigs, people still crowded around Him for healing, or just to touch Him or listen to what He said. I hovered nearby, so grateful and stunned by what had happened to me. I wanted nothing else from Him. I just wanted to sit nearby and *feel* the depth of the healing that had taken place inside me. My mind was calm. Whole. I was one person. Restored.

I was still sitting nearby when the leaders of our village marched out from town to confront Jesus. They headed toward Jesus. I was afraid they were going to hurt Him, and His disciples must have thought so, too, because they stood in front of Him to defend Him. But just as He had done with me, Jesus stepped right up to them as if they were friends. I was too far away to hear the full conversation—I was forgotten in all the commotion—but they begged Him to leave.

He did. Right then He and His men headed back toward their boat. I ran after them. I wanted to get on that boat with Him and be one of His followers. I would have done anything for Him. To Jesus, saving one man was worth the lives of all those pigs. Who would ever value me more than that?

I would have been the most devoted follower He ever had. But when I asked Him whether I could go with Him, He told me no. He wanted me to serve Him another way—by staying right where I was and telling everyone I knew what the Lord had done for me.

I was bitterly disappointed, but I obeyed. It wasn't easy. I went back to my family. I resumed my work. I told everyone what the Lord had done. Not everyone wanted to hear it. With Jesus gone, some of them blamed me for the pigs, and some of them still treated me with the same scorn as before.

I do the best I can day by day. I no longer want to die. I want to live, and with every breath I take from now and until the final breath leaves my body, I want to give thanks to the Lord who restored me.   —JB

//More than any other humiliation I suffered, the looks from other people were what I dreaded most and yet I couldn't blame them. To most of them I was a monster, not a human being.**//**

HIS PLACE IN GOD'S STORY

Healing people who were demon-possessed was an important part of Jesus' ministry. The Bible records more of those kinds of healings than any other type. As biblical scholar Paul W. Hollenbach points out, Jesus tied these healings from demon possession to His central theme of the coming of the kingdom of God. In Luke 11:20, Jesus says, "But if I drive out demons by the finger of God, then the kingdom of God has come to you" (NIV). He also identified driving out demons as a crucial task for His disciples when He sent them out to minister to people (Mark 3:15; Mark 6:7; Luke 9:1).

When Jesus healed people, He often told them to stay silent about it. For example, when Jesus healed the man with leprosy, He sent him away with a strong warning not to tell anyone (Mark 1:44). Despite Jesus' command, the man couldn't resist telling others what had happened to him. People often had trouble keeping quiet about the miracles Jesus performed.

However, the Gadarene demoniac's story is an exception to Jesus' more usual approach of asking for silence after a healing. The man wanted to get in the boat and go away with Jesus after he was healed, but Jesus refused because He had in mind a different way for the man to serve Him: "'Go home to your family and tell them how much the Lord has done for you, and how he has had mercy on you.' So the man went away and began to tell in the Decapolis how much Jesus had done for him. And all the people were amazed" (Mark 5:19-20, NIV). The Gadarene demoniac was a powerful witness for Jesus after his healing, but only because he set aside his own idea about the best way to follow Jesus and obeyed Jesus' particular calling for him instead.

THE STORY FINDS ITS PLACE IN ME

1. What parts of the Gadarene Demoniac's story find their place in you?

▼

2. Our culture no longer makes people live among the tombs, but are there modern-day equivalents for how we marginalize people? What part does Jesus now expect His followers to play in reaching those who have been tossed aside?

3. Once he is healed, the man wants to go with Jesus. Have you ever faced a situation in which you wanted to serve Jesus in one way, but He opened up opportunities for you to serve in a different way? Was it difficult for you to lay aside your own agenda in order to follow His? What was the result?

4. In what ways have you seen people changed because of Jesus'
   presence? Has He changed your own life? How?

5. Some in this story chose to focus on the loss of the pigs instead of the miracle of healing Jesus provided. Reflect on a time in your life when you've focused on the minute when God was doing something huge.

NOTES

▼

THE UNCLEAN WOMAN

THE FAITHFUL • KEY SCRIPTURE PASSAGE: Mark 5:21-43

HER CONTEXT

The book of Leviticus is thought to have been written between 1440 and 1400 BC and most presumably by Moses. And with 247 of the 613 rabbinical laws coming from it, it is one of the most exhaustive books. From Leviticus we can see not only how imperative cleanliness was, but who was affected and how. Women were no exception.

For a young Israelite woman growing up and living in ancient times, her first menstrual cycle would have been both a time of celebration, marking her as woman, and the beginning of a life of regular separation as she moved between "clean" and "unclean." During her cycle she was exempt from the usual heavy chore load of collecting water, serving food to her family, and going to the marketplace. If she was married, it was a time of abstinence from her spouse.

Leviticus is quite frank in marking women as being ceremonially unclean for seven days when they had their cycle. To bleed meant to be ceremonially unclean, to be divided from the religious practices that were so core to being Jewish then.

These were not peoples' opinions or ideologies, but matters that had been written into the Pentateuch, the very fabric of their being. To breach any of the intricate Levite laws was to isolate oneself and suffer lonely consequences.

Our unclean woman would have known herself to be a feared outcast. After twelve years of trying to buy any kind of healing to be accepted back, she would have been only too aware of what her presence in the crowd meant, and even more so, what touching a rabbi would result in.

It is impossible to overstate the overwhelming grief she would have endured, and the sheer suffering at being made intentionally invisible by her family, friends, and community.

HER STORY

"Do you want this or not, then?" a voice called. It is a loud voice, I would know, I only hear a few in this place.

Slowly I pull myself up; at least that's what I think I am doing. When I open my eyes to look down, I can see I'm not walking; I am crawling.

I reach the door lintel and pull my shawl further down my face.

"That's close enough," says the voice. It belongs to Dorit, Jeremiah's daughter.

I nod, but my eyes are fixed on the flattened loaves, barely wrapped in a cloth in her other hand.

She reaches out tentatively and puts the small parcel down.

"The rain was heavy last night, you are kind to have come," I say. That is an understatement. I thought the heavens were going to fall on top of us all. The skies were as dark and fury-filled as when Eli had come to me. He had screamed his new lungs empty and deafened the thunder. My mind stops on him. My oldest and youngest boy, who never knew my face. My boy, who I only held onto briefly before they took him, before they said I would taint him. My boy Eli, who I only saw from afar if he was playing outside or running errands.

"You should know," Dorit says, cutting in. "Elim is back. He is looking for you. He's told everyone you owe him more money and that if you don't return it, you're a thief."

A small sigh escapes me. I let my shawl fall back and lift my face.

"Then he should ask every doctor in Galilee where his money is."

Dorit nods shyly and hurries off back down the wheat-colored hill and to the dusty, rocky path to the kibbutz by the sea. My shoulders sag as her head disappears out of sight. I look over my small hut. The thatched roof is still dripping and leaving puddles on the dirt floor.

I watch the empty road. I hadn't even said thank you.

The sun is much higher in the sky when I leave the place. It has been so many years, but it is still simply "the place." As I walk I remember.

When we were first wed, my husband's sisters put dried rosebuds all over our bed. They got caught in my hair, but he wouldn't pick them out. I was his *vered,* his rose. He said they were jewels from nature and so I smelt like roses every day thereafter. When I was carrying Eli, he gave me a flower each morning. I would laugh at him, but he wouldn't stop. And then our real flower bloomed and our son was born and my life was torn from me in that room. Yet none of that pain compares with my husband's eyes the day he asked me to leave. He had never been one for charades.

The Sea of Galilee is nothing more than a lake, but to my village it is the ocean. The fishermen stay out there and, balancing on boat and land, yell their prices and throw their silver fish into baskets.

I walk along. I want to feel the Galilee breeze on my face. Someone is roasting tilapia, turning it over on its basting spoke whilst another is singing proudly. The song is about the winds and furious Leviathan who waits in the deepest part of our sea waiting for tired souls to swim over him.

I'm lucky. If I am quiet, I can sit here the whole afternoon on the water's edge and Elim can turn my hut over until its spills outside, for I have nothing left to give him.

A loud rumble and the rolling sound of repeated thuds interrupts my thoughts. I look up just in time to see a man in a beige tunic striding ahead of a scurrying crowd. His scarred arms are high about his head and his voice is loud and excited, like a child who has learned to talk.

"I am free because of the Rabbi! Gone are the graveyards and all their many voices. I am free because of Him!" He stops to tell the crowd, beaming proudly.

THE UNCLEAN WOMAN

I stand up slowly, feeling every creak and ache. I watch the faces of those looking at him. They aren't blank with disinterest or annoyed to have their morning broken up by his insistent yelling. And then I look at him. He looks familiar, which was impossible; I would never forget a head of red curls like that.

"It's Aviv, Gil's son," whispers one woman, loud enough for anyone nearby to hear.

"No! The one they kept chained with the tombstones?" another lady answers and visibly shivers.

"The very same," nods her friend. "He says that wandering wise man from Nazareth healed him. He fixed whatever was broken in his head."

"Never," gasped the other, clapping her hand on her cheek.

"Proof's right there. I don't think anyone has ever seen Aviv with this many clothes still on," said the first woman. "And then there's Kefir's pigs. The whole herd ran into the river and drowned after the Rabbi sent the bad spirits into them."

"No!"

"Oh, yes. Anyway, hurry, they say the Rabbi is here today. I have to ask Him . . ." Her voice trailed off with the moving crowd.

I hadn't realized that I had left the small sea wall and was following them. My head was full and at the same time it was completely empty with one thing left: the Rabbi.

* * *

He isn't difficult to spot. It isn't hard to be found in the villages and towns in the Decapolis; especially when every able-bodied person is pressing in around you.

The crowd is relentless in its shoving and pushing. People are stepping over each other and shouting to Him, calling Him; crying in some cases.

I stop in the entrance to Dalia's fabric shop. With one hand I try to press down the pain that is now strangling my lower back. I slide down the wall trying to breathe and do the things the doctors said I should, but all I can see is the pain: large and wide and flattening me.

Someone makes his way through the people. The crowd actually makes a gap for him. He stops in front of the Rabbi, gulping and stammering. All I can hear is "my daughter is dying."

I turn carefully and see Jairus weeping so hard that he's unrecognizable as the respectable synagogue leader he is. The Rabbi simply nods and follows him.

Perhaps later I will know when and how the notion caught me, but right now there is only the Rabbi and me.

I creep forward, hunched over so deeply most people don't notice how close they are to being unclean until sunset. My heart is in my ears; all I can hear is the silent thudding. I won't touch His actual skin—I can't—but just the tip of His dusty robe; just the edge.

It is swift. One moment I am in the deepest dark and then in a blink I am outside of it. I remember my mother telling me off for being superstitious, but all I can think now is that something so truly unusual and unnatural just happened.

There is no pain. There is nothing tearing up my body from the inside out anymore. I stand, pull my shawl down over my face, and start to slip back.

Maybe I make five paces and then He stops and turns. His eyes swiftly run over us all.

"Who touched me?" It was the first time He spoke, so the hush was instant. "Who touched my clothes?"[1]

One of the men with Him looks a little embarrassed and whispers something about the number of people here and the likelihood of finding a particular person.

But He still stares. It isn't a withering stare, but it is definitely a challenge.

We all wait in an awkward silence. Jairus looks perplexed and is wringing his fingers tightly.

Then His eyes find mine and stay there. I start walking forward without meaning to and then I am in a heap before Him. The shaking is uncontrollable. It is as if someone has just thrown me into the sea in December.

I keep my eyes closed. I don't want to see everyone's face. I don't want to see His. I talk and it's hurried. I tell Him why I did it before my mind switches on and seals my lips. Then I hear it spoken in the most careful of ways, so that no one else can hear.

"My daughter," He starts. Something in my core breaks and I do look up. He is smiling wide and his eyes are glassy.

"My daughter, your faith has healed you," He continues. "Go in peace, free from your suffering."

A messenger comes then and speaks to Jairus and the Rabbi and the crowd move on with them. I remain there on the ground with a few stragglers gaping and waiting to ask questions.

None of them matter. Today I was looked on kindly. Today, perhaps I can return to my own home and hold Eli; if he'll let me.

Today I was brought back.

—EL

HER PLACE IN GOD'S STORY

The unclean woman gets one mere paragraph in the Gospels of Mark and Luke, yet her suffering in those short lines is enough to have been used by pastors and public speakers alike ever since. Furthermore, ultimately it is Jesus himself who brings her to the forefront by highlighting her faith in Him.

What tends to stand out the most with this woman is that she bled continuously for twelve years. We can appreciate, though probably never fully understand, how cruelly she hurt. But perhaps we tend to overlook what this says about her. She had an indomitable spirit. To have outlasted twelve years of medical probing, spent everything, tolerated questioning and essentially been the subject of testing, by those who were never able to find a cure, speaks of the human spirit at its strongest (Mark 5:25-26).

This woman remained with hope. Unfathomably she did not become so calcified as to reject the news of this supposed healer. She would have heard the stories of what He had done, and she decided there was every chance He could do the same for her (Mark 5:27).

It is impossible to discuss the unclean woman without using the word "brave." She held on to life with barely any human contact and was confined into her own form of purgatory for something she had no control over. And yet when Jesus is calling out to the crowd for the "power taker" to come forth, whereas most would have endured the horribly long silence to save face, she exposed herself. She opened herself to the mercy of critics and fear mongers alike and she spoke up. It says she trembled and fell to her feet. She was terrified about what would happen next, but she did not hide (Mark 5:27-28).

Throughout the Gospels Jesus seems very appreciative and, quite frankly, surprised by honest people. When He asks the question of who touched His robe, she could have followed the logical but untrue line of being squashed in the crowd. Instead she lets everyone hear who she is and where she's been (Mark 5:32-33).

Although the whole exchange between this woman and Jesus appears to be very brief, He uses those few moments to call her one of His own: "daughter." He clears her name, declares her clean, and restores her to the community, understanding her survival depends upon it (Mark 5:34).

"I keep my eyes closed. I don't want to see everyone's face. I don't want to see His. I talk and it's hurried. I tell Him why I did it before my mind switches on and seals my lips. Then I hear it spoken in the most careful of ways, so that no one else can hear. 'My daughter . . .'"

THE STORY FINDS ITS PLACE IN ME

1. What parts of the Unclean Woman's story find their place in you?

2. The unclean woman has tried everything available to her. All of her resources—both financial and emotional—have been spent. Yet she still remains faithful in her hope for healing. Have you ever experienced this kind of tenacious faith?

3. Because of her condition she is overtly marginalized and feared. She has no support network, yet still rises to meet another day. Have you found yourself on the very edge of everything? Of family, friends, colleagues and found yourself unheard and not understood?

4. After she gets her miracle, the woman is absolutely terrified to the point of visibly shaking. For the first time the limelight is on her. Someone is waiting for her to speak, to share her side and as afraid as she is, she does it. Are you prepared to go headlong into your fear and overcome it with your earnestness?

5. For 12 years the unclean woman was obedient to the laws regarding her uncleanliness. Her decision to break the law now was a significant symbol of her audacious faith that Jesus would heal her. Write of a time you acted with this bold faith or write about what it would look like to do that in your life.

THE UNCLEAN WOMAN

NOTES

▼

 OTHER STUDIES IN THE NAMED SERIES:

The Patriarchs

The Disciples

The Women